W9-AXI-545

# THE
# HURON
# INDIANS

THE JUNIOR LIBRARY OF
AMERICAN INDIANS

# THE
# HURON
# INDIANS

*Martin Schwabacher*

CHELSEA JUNIORS

a division of CHELSEA HOUSE PUBLISHERS

FRONTISPIECE: A tray made of bark and decorated with dyed porcupine quills.

CHAPTER TITLE ORNAMENT: A drawing inspired by a Wendat pipe bowl.

English-language words that are italicized in the text can be found in the glossary at the back of the book.

**Chelsea House Publishers**

EDITORIAL DIRECTOR Richard Rennert
EXECUTIVE MANAGING EDITOR Karyn Gullen Browne
COPY CHIEF Robin James
PICTURE EDITOR Adrian G. Allen
CREATIVE DIRECTOR Robert Mitchell
ART DIRECTOR Joan Ferrigno
PRODUCTION MANAGER Sallye Scott

**The Junior Library of American Indians**

SENIOR EDITOR Martin Schwabacher

**Staff for THE HURON INDIANS**

EDITORIAL ASSISTANT Sydra Mallery
ASSISTANT DESIGNER Lydia Rivera
PICTURE RESEARCHER Villette Harris
COVER ILLUSTRATOR Hal Just

First Printing

1 3 5 7 9 8 6 4 2

**Library of Congress Cataloging-in-Publication Data**

Schwabacher, Martin.
The Huron Indians / Martin Schwabacher.
  p. cm. — (The Junior library of American Indians)
Includes index.
    0-7910-2489-X
    0-7910-2033-9 (pbk.)
1. Wyandot Indians—Juvenile literature. [1. Wyandot Indians.
2. Indians of North America.] I. Title. II. Series.
E99.H9S38 1995
398.2'089'975—dc20
94-34895
CIP
AC

# CONTENTS

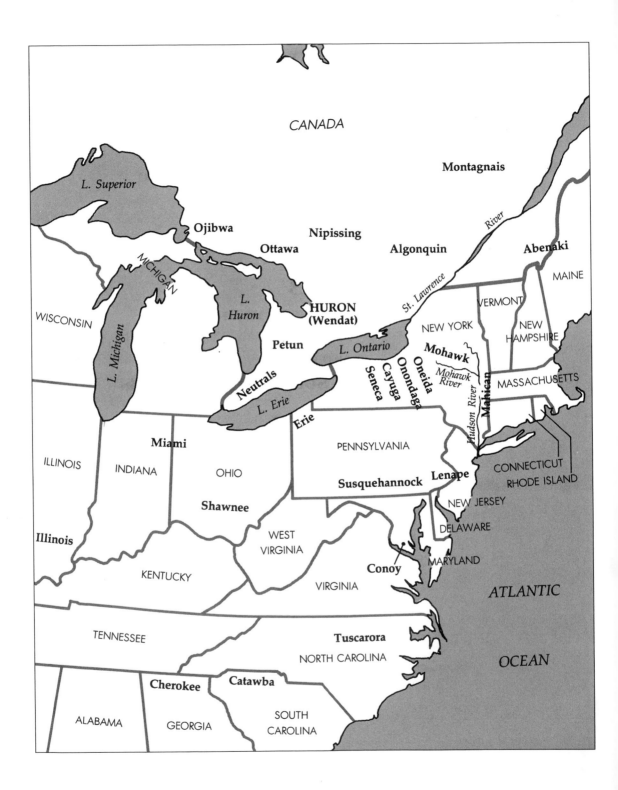

*Archaeologists believe that the ancestors of the Hurons settled in the region east of Lake Huron a thousand years before the first Europeans arrived in America.*

CHAPTER **1**

# On the Back of the Turtle

In Ontario, Canada, just to the east of Lake Huron, is the area that was once known as Huronia, the land of the Hurons. When the first Europeans reached Huronia in the early 1600s, there were about 20,000 Huron Indians living there. The Hurons were not actually a single tribe but a confederacy of four related tribes. Because these tribes acted together in matters of trade, war, and politics, they are spoken of as a single group.

Huron is the name that the French traders gave this group. It comes from a French word meaning "wild boar" or "savage." The Hurons' name for  themselves, however, is Wendat, meaning "people who live on an island or a *peninsula*."

Although the Hurons did not live on an island, their land was surrounded by water. The western part of their land was a peninsula jutting into Georgian Bay, which is part of Lake Huron. To the east was Lake Simcoe. Numerous streams crossed the Hurons' territory, and the land was dotted with small lakes.

The Hurons had another reason to call themselves islanders. According to their myth about the beginning of the world, all people live on the back of a giant turtle floating in the ocean.   At one time the world was covered with water. There were no people, but there were beings similar to humans who lived in the sky. One of these beings, a woman named Aataentsic (ah-TANT-sik), fell through a hole in the sky. She was caught by two loons who saved her from drowning. Because there was only water, the loons did not know what to do with the woman, so they called the other animals for help. Great Turtle told the birds to put the woman on his back. Other animals dove to the bottom of the sea and brought up dirt to put on Great Turtle's back, forming the earth.

Aataentsic was pregnant when she fell, and she soon gave birth to twin boys, Iouskeha (yoo-SKEE-ha) and Tawiscaron (da-WIS-ga-ron). Iouskeha was good, but Tawiscaron was so evil that when he was born he broke through his mother's side, killing her. After Aataentsic was buried, corn, beans, and squash grew from her grave. These became the Hurons' most important foods.

The brothers began to prepare the world for people. Iouskeha wanted to make life easy, so he made animals such as dogs, deer, elk, and buffalo to help people. Tawiscaron created dangerous creatures to torment human beings, including serpents, panthers, wolves, bears, and mosquitoes. All were of monstrous size—the mosquitoes were the size of turkeys. Tawiscaron also made a giant toad that swallowed all the fresh water in the entire world.

Iouskeha went to search for the water in the land where his brother lived. There he fought the giant beasts his brother had made. Although he could not destroy them, he left them small enough that humans could overcome them. When he found the toad, he cut it open and water flowed out, creating rivers.

Iouskeha wanted one side of each river to flow upstream and the other to flow

downstream so that it would be easier for people to travel by canoe. His brother disagreed and made the rivers flow in one direction only, adding dangerous rapids and whirlpools.

The brothers knew they would never agree on anything, so they decided to fight to the death. The winner would rule the world. Each told the other the one thing that could destroy him, and the battle began. Tawiscaron battered his brother mercilessly with a bag of corn, his only weakness. As Iouskeha lay dying, his mother's spirit came to him and

*The Hurons were eager to exchange goods with French traders, but their contact with the French would lead to the destruction of the Huron Confederacy.*

revived him. Iouskeha then seized a deer antler and killed the evil Tawiscaron. The spirit of the dead brother announced that he was going to the west to join his mother's spirit in the land of the dead. "Hereafter," he said, "all men will go to the west after death."

This story of the creation of the world was told by a 75-year-old Huron man in 1874. He finished by saying, "And so until the Christian *missionaries* came to our land, the spirits of dead Indians went to the far west and lived there."

The missionaries he spoke of came from France in the 17th century to teach the Indians the beliefs of Christianity. European traders also entered Huron territory, bringing many changes to the Indians' lives. They brought metal goods, such as pots and knives, to exchange for beaver furs. The fur trade brought new wealth to the Hurons, but the newcomers carried terrible diseases that wiped out huge numbers of the Native Americans. They also brought guns, which would lead to the final downfall of the Hurons.

Fortunately, the early French explorers and missionaries wrote down many of their observations of Huron life before it was destroyed. These records give us a glimpse of the way of life of this extraordinary people.

This drawing from Samuel
de Champlain's Voyages
to New France shows the
V-shaped traps used by
the Hurons to hunt deer.
The hunters made loud
noises to scare the animals
into the pen at the narrow
end of the trap, where
they could easily be
killed with spears.

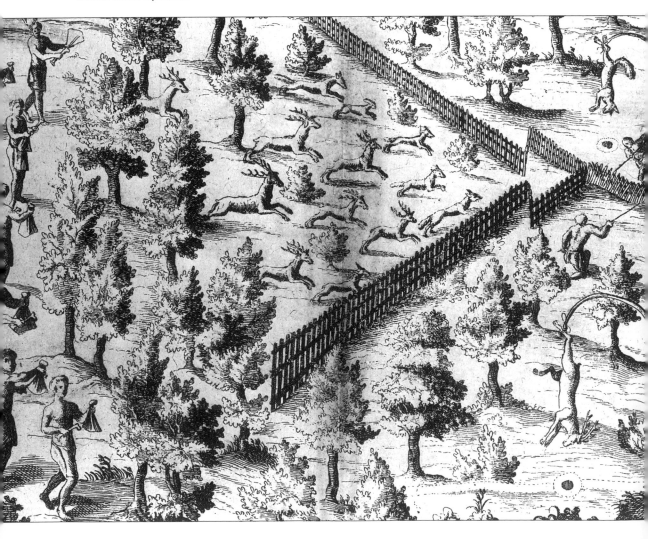

# CHAPTER 2

# Feeding the Body and Spirit

When the first missionaries arrived in Huronia, there were between 18 and 25 villages in the Huron Confederacy. The largest of these villages contained up to 2,000 people and were surrounded by high protective fences called palisades. These palisades were made of wooden poles about 15 feet high that were woven together with smaller branches. Tall watchtowers were built so that the Hurons could be on guard against attacks from their primary enemy, the Iroquois.

The villages were made up of *longhouses*, which were typically 90 to 100 feet long and 20 to 30 feet wide. A row of fireplaces, spaced about 20 feet apart, ran down the center of each house. One family lived on either side of each fireplace—if a house had four fireplaces, it housed eight families. Longhouses had no windows and were decorated on the outside with pictures, usually painted in red.

The floor of each longhouse was covered with bark, and there was a platform four or five feet off the ground to sit on or to sleep on in the summer. In the winter, the people slept on the floor near the fire to keep warm. There were holes in the roof to let out smoke from the fireplaces, but it was still so smoky indoors that older people sometimes got eye diseases, and some even went blind. Because the walls of the longhouses were made of bark, there was a constant danger of fire, so the Hurons protected their most important possessions by burying them.

The Hurons produced most of their food by farming, which was done by the women. Before crops could be planted, the men had to clear fields from the forest, chopping down the smaller trees with stone axes and burning the bigger trees. The soil in the fields ran out of nutrients after 10 or 12 years of planting, so the men were constantly clearing new fields. The women prepared the fields and

*Huron women placed dried corn kernels into a hollowed-out tree stump (left) and ground them into flour using a wooden pole (right).*

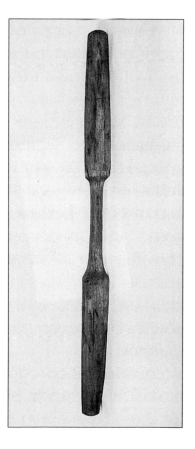

planted the seeds. Throughout the summer the women and children tended the fields, keeping them free of weeds and scaring away the birds, raccoons, and numerous other animals that feasted on the crops. In autumn, the women harvested the crops and prepared them to be stored for the winter.

Corn was the most important food for the Hurons. The most common dish was a soup made from cornmeal, which the women made by putting dried corn kernels in a hollowed-out tree stump and pounding them with a pole. Slices of fish, meat, or squash might be added to the soup; or a fish might be boiled, pounded into a mash, and returned to the soup. Little cakes of cornmeal bread were baked in the ashes of the fireplace. The women sometimes made a special bread by chewing up fresh corn, spitting it out, wrapping the paste in corn leaves, and baking it. *Leindohy*, which means "stinky corn," was made by letting small ears of corn ferment in a pool of water for several months. The French were disgusted by leindohy and complained that their fingers smelled for several days if they so much as touched it.

In addition to corn, the Hurons planted beans and squash. Sunflowers were grown for the oil that could be squeezed from their seeds. The Indians added this oil to their food and rubbed it on their bodies to protect their skin from the wind and cold weather. Although Huron men grew small patches of tobacco near their homes, most of their tobacco was acquired through trade with the tribes to the south, where it grew more easily.

The main source of meat was fish, which were caught with nets or wooden spears. During the winter, men fished by cutting holes through the ice. Fish that was not eaten right away was dried or smoked so that it could be stored for future use.

Huron men hunted birds and game with nets, traps, and bows and arrows. They also trained dogs to help them track bears, which the men shot with arrows. Hunting provided the Hurons with some of their food, but it was more important as a source of animal skins, which were needed to make clothing.

The Hurons had an effective method for hunting deer that required several hundred men working together. All of the available hunters from a village would form a giant line or V shape and march forward, cornering the animals at a bend in a river, where they would be shot with arrows or speared from canoes. Another technique required building a V-shaped trap. The sides of these traps were nine feet high and a half-mile long.

Hunters beat sticks together to scare the deer and drive them into the point of the V, where they were shot with arrows.

Hunting was difficult in Huronia itself because there were so many people living in a relatively small area—the Hurons' homeland was only about 35 miles wide from east to west and 20 miles from north to south. By the 17th century, there were few animals left in the region. Groups of hunters had to travel a month or more to bring back meat and skins.

The Hurons also acquired skins by trading. They grew a great deal more corn than they needed to survive, and they traded the surplus with the tribes to the north, such as the Nipissing and the Ottawa. From these tribes the Hurons obtained furs and warm winter clothing. The northern hunters, who lived in a colder climate than the Hurons, knew how to make excellent clothing and camping equipment, and the clothes they made were often beautifully embroidered with dyed porcupine quills.

A typical Huron family had about three children. After a Huron woman had a child, she always waited at least two or three years before having another. Mothers pierced their babies' ears soon after they were born. During the day, infants were kept on cradle-boards—flat pieces of wood that allowed

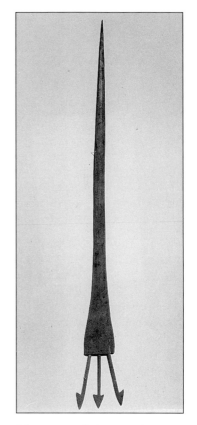

*The many lakes and rivers of Huronia provided an important part of the Hurons' diet. Men caught fish with nets or with wooden spears such as this one.*

mothers to carry their babies on their backs. The cradleboards were decorated with paintings and strings of beads. Soft fluff, probably from the cattail plant, was used for diapers.

As they grew older, children spent their time playing games and learning the skills they would need as adults. Boys practiced shooting arrows and throwing fishing spears. Young girls were taught to pound corn and to help their mothers with their work. The French missionaries noted with displeasure that Huron children were never spanked or beaten. At that time in France, children were raised very strictly. They were taught to fear and obey their parents. The Hurons' lack of *domineering* parental figures was hard for the French to understand. But Huron children knew that their families would be disappointed in them if they misbehaved. The fear of letting down their families encouraged the children to act appropriately.

People were accountable not only to their immediate family but to a larger group of relatives called a clan. There were eight clans: Turtle, Wolf, Bear, Beaver, Deer, Hawk, Porcupine, and Snake. Clans cut across tribal and village lines, so each person had relatives in many different villages. This helped unify Huron society and prevent warfare. Because people were not allowed to marry someone from their own clan, each marriage formed further bonds between different groups.

Children were members of their mother's clan, not their father's. This meant that a man was more closely related to his sister's children than to his own children, because his nieces and nephews were in his clan, while his children were not.

Young men and women in Huron society could have as many girlfriends or boyfriends as they wanted. When a man decided that he wanted to marry, he asked the woman's parents for permission to propose. If her parents consented, the man would paint his face and bring the woman a present such as a necklace or a beaver robe. The two would spend several nights together, during which they were not allowed to speak. After this period, the girl would announce whether she wanted to marry her suitor, keeping his gift regardless of her decision. If she agreed to the marriage, the wedding was celebrated with a feast provided by her father.

The Hurons believed that no one should be forced to do anything against his or her will, and this included staying married. Either partner in a marriage could leave the other at any time, and divorce was common. After

*This 17th-century sketch shows the clothing worn by Huron women. During the summer they wore skirts made of deer or beaver skins. In colder weather, they also wore leggings and wrapped skins around their upper bodies. Both men and women adorned their bodies with strands of shell beads.*

a couple had a child, however, they rarely separated.

Huron society was devoted to making sure that the needs of all of its members were taken care of. No one went hungry as long as anyone had food to share, and the Hurons' skill at farming ensured that there was usually plenty for all. Even more important to the Hurons than their physical needs, however, were their spiritual needs.

The Hurons' views on spirituality were startlingly different from the Europeans'. Fortunately, the Christian missionaries who lived among the Hurons in the 17th century kept detailed records of their attempts to *convert* the Indians to Christianity. These records reveal much about the way the Hurons saw the world. The Hurons believed that the world was filled with spirits, and that these spirits influenced every aspect of their lives. ▲

CHAPTER **3**

# People of the Dream

One of the things that most amazed Jean de Brébeuf, a *Jesuit* priest who went to live among the Hurons in 1631, was the immense importance the Indians placed on dreams. Brébeuf observed that to the Hurons, dreams were seen as orders that had to be obeyed immediately. A dream, he wrote in 1636, "predicts to them future events" and guides their every act. "It prescribes their feasts, their dances, their songs, their games, in a word, the dream does everything and is in truth the principal god of the Hurons."

The Hurons believed that the things they saw and the beings they met in dreams really existed. Spirits lived in everything around them: corn, rocks, animals, even the sky. These spirits communicated with the Hurons through dreams, and they were too powerful to be disobeyed.

Father Francesco Bressani, another Catholic missionary, saw a Huron man cut off his own finger with a seashell because of a dream. In the dream, the man had been captured by a hostile tribe who was cutting off his finger. The only way he could prevent the dream from coming true, he believed, was to cut off the finger himself.

This obedience to dreams frightened some of the missionaries who visited the Indians of the Northeast. "What peril we are in every day," wrote one Jesuit priest, "among people who will murder us in cold blood if they have dreamed of doing so." At least one Huron did dream about killing a French priest. "I killed a Frenchman; that is my dream. Which must be fulfilled at any cost," the man insisted. He finally agreed to accept a coat from the body of a dead Frenchman as a substitute for an actual killing.

Spirits often gave people advice in dreams. For instance, a person might be taught a song or be shown an object to use as a magic charm. Charms could make one lucky in hunting, fishing, trading, fighting, gambling, and love. These charms were extremely valuable and were passed down through the generations.

Dreams told people when to hold their feasts, dances, and other important ceremonies, and how to perform them. One traditional ritual began when the spirit of a fishing net appeared to a man in a dream. The spirit asked the man for a new bride to replace the wife he had lost. In response to

*This rattle, made of a deer horn, deerskin, and feathers, was used during dances.*

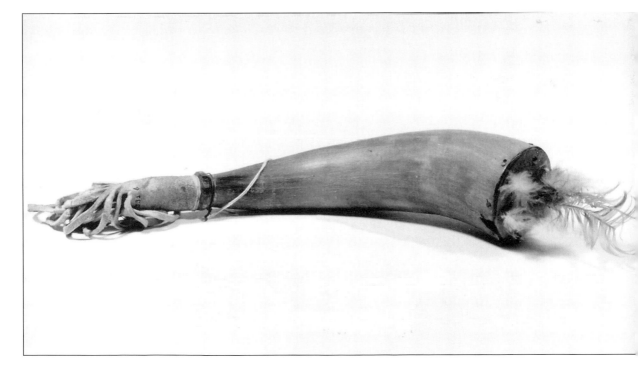

that dream, a ceremony was performed in which two young girls were married to a fishing net. Providing wives for the nets was believed to bring good luck in fishing, so the Hurons continued to hold the ceremony regularly. The marriages lasted for one year, after which the girls were free to marry someone else.

Some of the most important messages the Hurons received in dreams came from parts of their own souls that they were aware of only while they were asleep. Paying extremely close attention to these messages was considered crucial to one's spiritual and physical health. In 1649, Father Paul Ragueneau, a French missionary, wrote this description of the Hurons' beliefs about the secret desires of the soul:

> In addition to the desires which we generally have that are free, or at least voluntary in us . . . the Hurons believe that our souls have other desires, which are, as it were, inborn and concealed. These, they say, come from the depths of the soul. . . . Now they believe that our soul makes these natural desires known by means of dreams, which are its language. Accordingly, when these desires are accomplished, it is satisfied; but, on the contrary, if it be not granted what it desires, it becomes angry, and not only does not give its body the good and the happiness that it wished to procure for it, but often it also revolts against the body, causing various diseases, and even death. . . . Most of the Hurons are very care-

ful to note their dreams, and to provide the soul
with what it has pictured to them during their
sleep. If, for instance, they have seen a javelin in
a dream, they try to get it; if they have dreamed
that they gave a feast, they will give one on awak-
ening, if they have the wherewithal; and so on
with other things. And they call this *Ondinnonk*—a
secret desire of the soul manifested by a dream.

These beliefs seemed incredible to
Europeans in the 17th century, but over 200
years after this was written the great Austrian
psychoanalyst Sigmund Freud developed
similar ideas. Freud claimed that people
have hidden memories and desires, which
can cause physical problems. He believed
that these thoughts come to people in their
dreams in a disguised form. Freud had his
patients tell him their dreams so that he could
figure out their hidden meanings.

The Hurons also believed that dreams
could have hidden meanings. If the meaning
of a dream was unclear, the dreamer would
ask for help in understanding his hidden
desires. Certain people, who were believed
to have great spiritual power, could communicate with the spirit of the dreamer in
order to understand his or her secret desire.

When the needs of a sick person's soul
became known, the villagers did all they
could to satisfy that wish. The Hurons placed
great importance on generosity, so it was

considered an honor to attend to such a need. A sick person might be offered hundreds of gifts from everyone in the village, all hoping that their gift would be the one to restore his health.

When an important person was ill, or if many people were sick or unhappy, a village chief might call for a special ceremony known as *Ononharoia* (o-non-ha-RO-ya), which means "turning the brain upside down." The ritual could also be held if an important member of the village received a message in a dream calling for it. The Ononharoia was held at least once every winter.

*Pictured here is a modern reconstruction of a longhouse. Because the longhouses were built of wooden poles and tree bark, they could easily catch fire.*

The Ononharoia ceremony lasted three days. On the first day, everyone who felt out of sorts would gather in groups in the evening and go from house to house, singing and shouting. They entered each house and began knocking things over, breaking clay pots, and throwing around burning pieces of wood from the fire. Because the Hurons' longhouses were made of wood and bark, a house would sometimes catch on fire.

On the second day, the visitors returned and announced that they had each had a dream. The villagers would shower them with gifts, such as kettles, knives, pipes, dogs, skins, fish, and tobacco. All hoped that they would be the lucky one who guessed the proper gift called for by the dream. The visitors would give hints about the dream in the form of a riddle. For instance, one person who dreamed of a pumpkin or a squash hinted, "What I want and see is that which bears a lake in itself," referring to the pumpkin's watery center. Another person said, "What I see in my eyes, it will be marked with various colors." The Huron word for "eye" also means "glass bead," so whoever solved this riddle correctly would offer some colorful glass beads. When a person finally received the correct gift, he or she would shout with joy, thank the giver, and run out of the house. Everyone who saw this would shout "Hey-ey-ey-ey-ey!" and strike the ground with their hands to celebrate, because this meant that the sufferer would be cured.

At the conclusion of the Ononharoia, the participants would go into the forest and return free of their maladies. They would then return all the presents they had been given except the ones that had fulfilled their dreams.

The Hurons had many other rituals, including feasts and dances, that helped bind them together as a community. Perhaps the most important was the Feast of the Dead, held every 10 years, during which the bones of the dead people from several villages were mixed together in a common grave. These ceremonies played an important role in maintaining peace and unity among the 20,000 people who made up the Huron Confederacy.

Huron society depended on all members demonstrating courtesy, generosity, and self-control; it was a matter of pride and honor to maintain these qualities. The opposite qualities were valued when dealing with enemies. Against members of enemy tribes, such as the Seneca and other members of the hated Iroquois Confederacy, the Hurons committed gruesome acts of violence. For an outsider, it is difficult to understand how people who would not hesitate to give away everything they owned to their neighbors could also regularly perform horrible acts of ritual torture. Part of the explanation lies in the Hurons' complex philosophy about the nature of the human soul. ◣

Father Francesco
Bressani, who lived
with the Hurons in 1643,
drew these images of
village life. Pictured are
a woman grinding corn
and a group of men
torturing a prisoner.

# CHAPTER 4

# War Souls and
# Peace Souls

The Hurons believed that their souls were made up of many different parts, each with a different function. Various parts of the soul took over at different times: Some were active while a person slept, and others were active while one was awake. One soul was in control when a person was angry, another during periods of calm reflection.

The different parts of the soul included the *eiachia*, which represented the heart or emotions; the *yaata*, the body soul; and the *onnhekwi*, or general life soul. These souls were connected to the body. The intellectual soul or mind, which was called the *yandiyonra*,

33

*This Huron warrior arms himself with arrows and a large shield made of cedar bark.*

and the free soul, or *oki*, were not bound to the body. The word oki was also used to describe nonhuman spirits.

When a brave person died, the Hurons might eat his heart and drink his blood in order to acquire some of his spirit. The same reasoning applied to eating foods such as corn. By eating corn, a person strengthened her own oki by bringing the oki of the corn into her body. Herbs that were used to cure disease were believed to contain an oki that healed the oki of the sick person. Smoking tobacco was considered a mingling of one's spirit with the spirit of the tobacco.

Hunting was possible only because the animal spirits allowed the hunters to capture their bodies. For this reason, the Hurons were careful not to burn the bones of animals they had caught; they thought that this would anger the animal spirits, who would make it harder for the hunters to catch them in the future. Father Ragueneau wrote in 1652 that if the "Hurons while hunting have some difficulty in killing a bear or a stag, and on opening it they find in its head or in its entrails something unusual, such as a stone or a snake, they will say that this is an *Oky*, and that it is what gave the animal such strength, and prevented it from dying; and they will take that stone or snake for a charm, and believe that it will bring them good fortune."

The human oki was similar to the oki of nonhuman things. A person's oki was active during sleep, when it would leave the body and communicate with other oki. This activity was experienced as dreams. It was the oki that gave information about charms or what was needed to heal the body. That is one reason why dreams were so important; they could contain messages from the dreamer's oki or from other spirits.

The intellectual soul also left the body, but this could happen while a person was awake. The Hurons believed that when a person thought about an object, the mind left the body and went to that object. That explained why one could imagine or "see" something in the mind that was not present. This experience was similar to having one's "mind wander." To the Hurons, the mind really had wandered, right out of the body.

In contrast to the intellectual soul was the eiachia, the heart. This soul was connected to one's body and feelings. Usually when a person was awake, the intellectual soul was in control. But when a person experienced very strong emotions, the eiachia took over.

*continued on page 45*

# HURON EMBROIDERY

The Huron embroidery on the following pages displays a combination of European techniques and traditional methods. In 1639, French nuns taught young Huron girls to embroider with imported thread. When the foreign materials ran out, the artists switched to moosehair. Small bunches of colored moosehair were sewn with sinew onto leather coats and moccasins.

By the 19th century, the Hurons were making embroidered clothing in workshops to sell to whites. Men cut up the leather and women did the sewing. Embroidery patterns became simpler so the goods could be made faster. Today, some Hurons still sell moccasins and other traditional products, but they are now decorated with glass beads instead of embroidery.

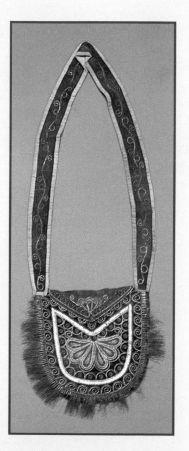

*Leather pouch and carrying strap made by the Hurons in Lorette in about 1830. Both are embroidered with dyed moosehair.*

The back (above) and front (below) of a sealskin hat, coat, and leggings, made in about 1780. This suit, which was probably owned by a Huron chief, is decorated with embroidered red cloth panels sewn to the skin. The human heads and animals on the back of the coat and the front of the leggings represent characters in a traditional Huron story.

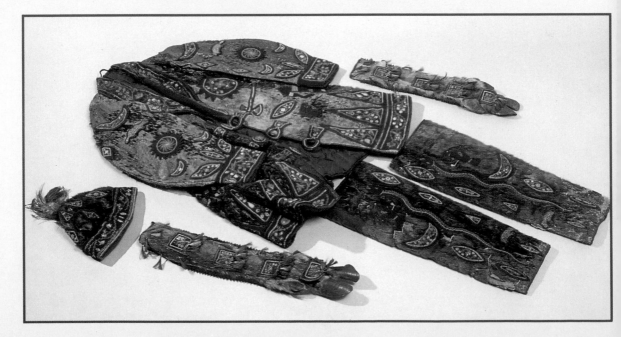

*Deerskin coat, made in about 1839. Styled like a 19th-century European army officer's coat, this garment is embroidered at the collar and cuffs with porcupine quills, a material particularly popular with Iroquois artisans.*

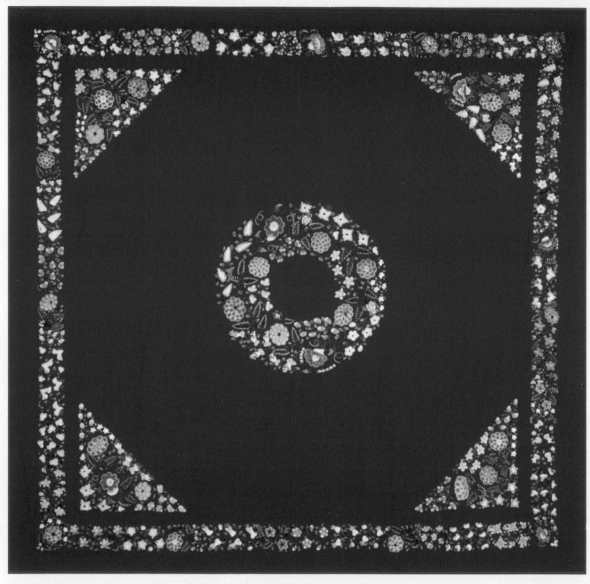

*Wool tablecloth, 6' x 5'8'', made in about 1860. This item is constructed from three layers of cloth sewn together at the sides with silk ribbon. The embroidered upper piece is backed with a thin piece of birchbark to hold in place the strands of moosehair that have been threaded through the cloth. Each stitch was made with a single strand of hair.*

Above: *Embroidered cloth and birch-bark novelty, 2½'' wide, made in 1850. The Huron sewed trinkets such as this for sale in Europe.*

Right: *Cloth eyeglass case embroidered with moosehair appliqué, made in 1840.*

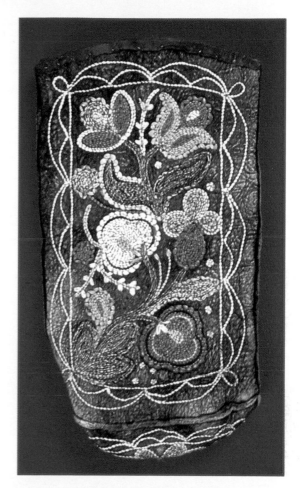

*Embroidered birch-bark container, 4'' x 2½'', made in about 1850. The Huron's decorative boxes, which they often embroidered with brown and green moosehair, were greatly valued by European traders.*

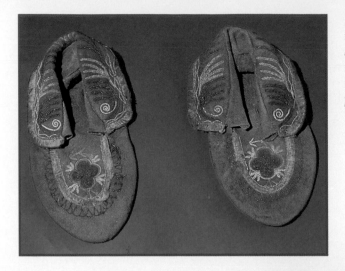

*Embroidered moccasins, each 10'' long, made in the late 1800s. The relative simplicity of the design on these shoes is typical of the embroidery produced by the Huron workshops during this period.*

**Below and right:** *Pairs of tanned leather moccasins, each shoe 10½'' long, made in about 1840. The Huron often dyed skins black to create a contrast with their multicolored moosehair appliqué.*

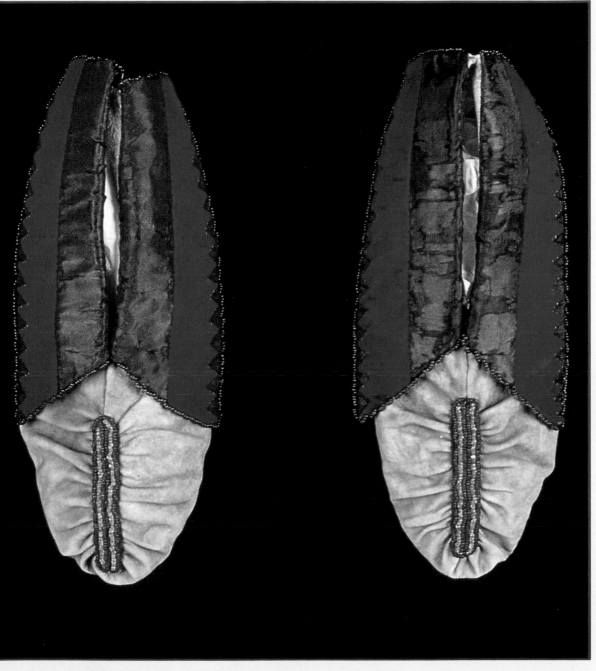

*Women's leather moccasins, each 9½'' long, made in 1912. Decorated with rows of beads and red tafetta ankle flaps, these shoes were crafted by Maggie Coon, a Wyandot woman, for wear during summer festivals. Unlike the Huron in Lorette, the Wyandot did not manufacture moccasins for sale.*

*Tanned leather moccasins, each 10" long, made in about 1780. Constructed by Huron in Detroit, this pair is decorated with dyed porcupine quills and glass beads.*

*Deerskin moccasin, 10" long, made in about 1840. The shoe is adorned with leather fringe and a variety of items the Huron obtained through trade: tubular glass beads made to imitate wampum (Indian shell beads); globular glass ornaments known as pony beads; and small pieces of tin.*

*continued from page 36*

The eiachia made one behave with great anger, great bravery, or both. During times of peace, the Hurons placed considerable value on calm, thoughtful behavior and patience. But during war, the qualities of the emotional soul became most important.

Just as each person had a soul for peace and a soul for war, each village had two chiefs, one for peace and one for war. A peace chief had to be intelligent, thoughtful, and calm. He had to be someone who did not get angry easily, even when insulted. According to an Indian saying, a peace chief should have skin "seven thumbs thick," so that nothing would bother him.

A war chief, on the other hand, had to be a vengeful warrior. Scholar John Steckley wrote that bravery and anger "were the two fundamental characteristics of a good warrior, that he be fearless in battle, unflinching when captured; and that he be ruthless in his anger for revenge (the main cause of war and raiding) in the practice of killing, capturing, and torturing members of enemy tribes."

There were separate meeting places for councils of peace and councils of war. Peace councils were held in the *endionrra ondaon*, "the place of the intellectual soul." War councils were held in the *otinontsiskiaj ondaon*, which meant "the house of cut-off heads."

Huron meetings were run by consensus, meaning that everyone had to agree to any decison. In Huron society, there were no rulers that people had to obey. No one could tell anyone else what to do. Chiefs were selected by the older women in the village and could be removed if they were unsatisfactory. When a decision had to be made that affected the whole group, the Huron leaders met and discussed the issue until all agreed on what to do. This was true whether the decision concerned a village, a tribe, or the entire confederacy.

At meetings of the Huron Confederacy, leaders from all the villages gathered in one longhouse. Before any meeting started, everyone sat together silently for a long time, smoking tobacco. Finally the subject of the meeting was announced. Each group discussed the issue among themselves, and then a spokesman would announce that group's opinion, slowly and formally. Each speaker would first repeat the subject being discussed, then state what each speaker before him had said. Each speech ended with the words, "that is my thought on the subject." All present would then exclaim "haau," saying it especially loud if they liked what had been said. Everyone remained calm and polite even if there was serious disagreement. Discussions could continue late into the night until a consensus was reached.

Personal freedom and the right to make one's own decisions were considered essential in Huron society. There were no laws or police force, but all people were responsible for showing self-control and respect for one another. Only in this way could they win the respect of their families, clans, and fellow villagers.

The threat of dishonor and criticism from one's family and neighbors was enough to deter most crime. If someone persisted in offending people, he could be kicked out of his family's longhouse and scorned by the other villagers.

The French missionaries were shocked by the lack of punishment for wrongdoers. But they admitted that there was much more crime in Europe, where order was maintained with police, prisons, public beatings, and hangings. Father Gabriel Lalemant wrote in 1645 that "in those practices which among (the Huron) are regarded as evil acts and are condemned by the public, we find without comparison much less disorder than there is in France, though here the mere shame of having committed the crime is the offender's punishment."

When a person from one clan killed some-one from another clan, the two clans would resolve the matter by agreeing on a payment to the victim's clan. Everyone in the murderer's clan would contribute equally to the gift, which was distributed to the victim's clan at a formal ceremony. Because a criminal's entire family shared his punish-ment, there was always pressure from one's relatives to behave properly.

This system of formal payment and apol-ogy helped prevent continual violence and revenge among members of the Huron Con-federacy. Against their enemies, however, the Hurons' revenge could be brutal. War against neighboring tribes, particularly the five tribes that made up the Iroquois Con-federacy, was a constant feature of Huron life.

The Hurons' principal enemies were the Senecas—the Iroquois tribe closest to them. A *blood feud* between the Hurons and the Senecas went on for at least 50 years, during which each side continued to seek revenge for previous killings. At the funerals of vic-tims, war chiefs would demand that the at-tackers be punished, and the families of the dead would give presents to the chiefs to encourage them to seek vengeance.

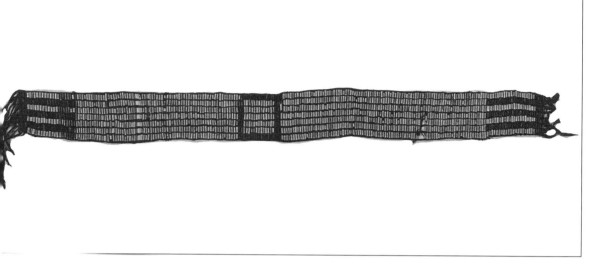

*The Huron Confederacy presented this wampum belt to the Iroquois Nation in 1612 to commemorate a peace treaty between the two groups. In spite of attempts to end fighting, the longtime enemies could not remain at peace for long.*

Young men were eager to prove their bravery and win respect by participating in war parties. Every year about 500 men traveled into Iroquois territory to commit raids. Huron warriors fought with wooden clubs and bows and arrows. They protected themselves with wooden shields and covered parts of their bodies with armor made of thin strips of wood. The symbol of their village or tribe was painted on a flag made of bark, and this was carried into battle.

Sometimes a large group would surround an enemy village for a week or more. Often, however, the war party would separate into small bands of five or six men. They would hide in fields or along paths in order to catch people whom they could take prisoner.

Sometimes captives would be killed immediately. These people were fortunate, because those who were taken back to Huronia would be tortured.

If a group of Huron warriors caught a lone enemy they would surround him and say quietly, "Sit down." They would then recite the cruel deeds his people had committed and that the Hurons were going to avenge by torturing him. The prisoner would bravely sing his war song as they marched back to Huron territory.

At home, the Huron chiefs would decide who got the honor of receiving the prisoner. An important family that had lost a relative to the Iroquois would adopt him to symbolically replace the dead person. Occasionally the prisoner would be welcomed into the family permanently, even receiving the name of the person he had replaced. Most of the time, however, this was a temporary ritual and would not prevent the captive from later being tortured to death. Women and children who were taken captive, however, usually became permanent members of their new families.

Before the torture began, the prisoner was given a farewell feast similar to that which a Huron would give if he thought he was about to die. He would sing and dance with the

Hurons, never showing that he feared death. The torture itself involved cutting and burning his flesh and could go on for several days.

If the prisoner was especially brave, the Hurons would perform certain rituals to gain some of his courage. For instance, they would cut out his heart, roast it, and eat it. By this means, the prisoner's strength and bravery was thought to enter their own bodies.

These ritual killings were performed with as much self-control and religious formality as was shown in their calm and peaceful council meetings. Whether in war or in peace, all of the Hurons' behavior was carefully calculated to insure harmony with the powerful forces and spirits that controlled their world. Nothing could protect them, however, from the powerful forces that would be unleashed when traders and explorers began arriving from France. ◣

CHAPTER 5

# The French

The French began trading with the Indians of New France, which is now Canada, in 1534, when the explorer Jacques Cartier led an expedition up the St. Lawrence River. He met hunters from several tribes who offered beaver pelts in exchange for cheap trade goods from Europe. Beaver fur was highly prized in Europe, where it was made into warm clothing and hats. The great demand for beaver furs led hundreds of Europeans to seek out Indian trading partners throughout North America.

The Hurons probably first acquired European items from their trading partners to the north. From tribes such as the Nipissing, the Hurons obtained French clothing, beads, and metal tools such as knives and cooking pots. The Hurons preferred the new metal tools to their clay pots and stone arrowheads and hatchet blades, so they were eager to begin trading with the French in person.

Their first direct contact with the French was probably their 1609 meeting with the explorer Samuel de Champlain. Because of their interest in the new metal trade goods, the Hurons called Champlain's party *agnon-ha*, which means "the iron people."

The Iroquois also wanted to trade with Champlain. He preferred to deal with the Hurons and the more northern tribes, however, because the beaver furs were thicker in areas with colder winters. To improve relations with the Hurons, Champlain promised not to trade with the Iroquois. He also agreed to join the Hurons in battles against their Iroquois enemies.

The first such joint raid came in 1609 against the Mohawks, one of the tribes in the Iroquois Confederacy. With the help of the French, the Hurons easily overcame the enemy. The Mohawks had never seen guns before, and the loud explosions and instant deaths of their comrades terrified them.

Champlain fought alongside the Hurons in several other battles, but their tactics baffled and frustrated him. He was used to having his orders obeyed absolutely, but as he wrote in his 1632 book, *Voyages to New France*, the Hurons "will have no discipline nor correction, and will do only what they please." Champlain complained that "the chiefs have in fact no absolute control over their men, who are governed by their own will and follow their own fancy, which is the cause of their disorder and the ruin of all their undertakings."

Champlain did not understand that the Hurons had very different goals in warfare than he did. He assumed that they wanted to achieve a total victory and conquer the Iroquois village being attacked. The Hurons, however, were more interested in demonstrating their bravery and punishing the enemy for previous raids.

To increase goodwill and understanding between the Hurons and the French, Champlain arranged for a Frenchman, Étienne Brulé, to live in a Huron village and study the language. Champlain also invited a Huron man to go with him to France and meet King Louis XIII. The Indian man was given a French name, Savignon, and was received politely at the royal court.

Savignon was not impressed by what he saw in France. He was shocked to see

parents hitting their children, prisoners being beaten, and people begging for food in
the streets, none of which had any place in
Huron life. Even public arguments offended
him.

The Catholic missionaries were likewise
horrified by certain aspects of Huron culture—such as the practice of *cannibalism*—
but they acknowledged that in some ways
Huron society was better than their own.
Gabriel de Sagard, a missionary who visited
Huronia in 1622–23, observed in his journal
that the Hurons were always extremely
generous, even with strangers:

> Whenever we had to go from one village to
> another for some necessity or business we used
> to go freely to their dwellings to lodge and get our
> food, and they received us in them and treated
> us very kindly although they were under no
> obligation to us. For they hold it proper to help
> wayfarers and to receive among them with polite-
> ness anyone who is not an enemy, and much
> more so those of their own nation. They recipro-
> cate hospitality and give such assistance to one
> another that the necessities of all are provided for
> without there being any indigent beggar in their
> towns and villages; and they considered it a very
> bad thing when they heard it said that there were
> in France a great many of these needy beggars,
> and thought that this was for lack of charity in us,
> and blamed us for it severely.

The missionaries went to New France with
good intentions. They risked their lives to

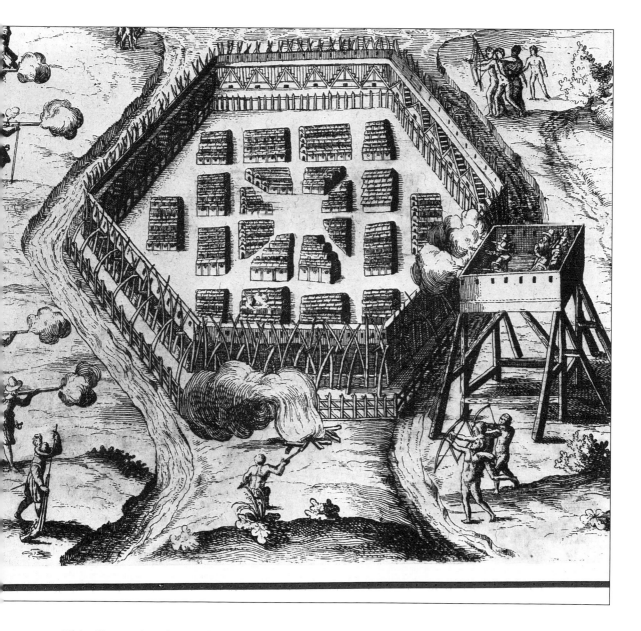

This illustration from Champlain's Voyages to New France shows Champlain's troops fighting alongside the Hurons in an attack on an Iroquois village in 1615.

bring their religion to the Hurons, believing that it would benefit the Indians. Unfortunately, the biggest change they brought was their unintentional introduction of diseases from Europe. The results were disastrous for the Hurons. Because they had never before faced diseases such as smallpox and measles, their bodies had no resistance to them. Almost everyone who caught these illnesses died. Disease swept through the Huron villages, killing thousands of people. In a series of epidemics from 1635 to 1640, the Huron population dropped from 20,000 to 10,000: half of the entire population had died in a five-year period.

The Hurons observed that the people who spent the most time with the missionaries were most likely to die. At that time neither the Indians nor the Europeans understood how diseases spread from one person to another. Some of the Hurons concluded that the missionaries were killing them with witchcraft. Father Lalemant wrote of the Hurons' feelings toward the French at this time:

> No doubt, they said, it must needs be that we had a secret understanding with the disease (for they believe that it is a demon), since we alone were all full of life and health, although we constantly breathed nothing but a totally infected air. Wherein truly it must be acknowledged that these

poor people are in some sense excusable. For it has happened very often, that where we were most welcome, where we baptized most people, there it was in fact where they died the most.

Many of the Hurons did not want the missionaries to remain in Huronia. They were allowed to stay, however, partly because they had converted a few *influential* families to Christianity. Although few Hurons were impressed by Catholicism, many chose to convert because the French paid Christian Indians more for furs than they paid non-Christians. After 1641, Christian Indians were also allowed to buy guns.

There was a more important reason that the priests were accepted by the Hurons: the French had threatened to cut off trade if the missionaries were forced to leave. The Hurons could not give up the fur trade. They had become dependent on the French for many of the things they needed, such as metal knives and pots. Many Hurons no longer knew how to make pots and knives out of clay and stone.

The Hurons had killed most of the beavers in their own territory by around 1630. Taking advantage of their good relations with the French, the Hurons continued to *prosper* by acquiring furs from neighboring tribes in exchange for corn and beans and a few French products. They would then trade those furs to the French in exchange for more French goods.

While the Hurons had been trading with the French, the Iroquois had been trading with the Dutch. Like the Hurons, the Iroquois quickly used up all the beavers in their territory. They also sought to acquire more furs from other tribes, leading to further fighting with the Hurons. Mohawk warriors began *ambushing* Huron traders on their way to French trading posts. These attacks made it difficult for the Hurons to continue their all-important trade.

After 1642, the Iroquois began making direct assaults on Huron villages. They attacked women working in the fields so often that the women became afraid to plant or harvest crops. Soon the Hurons, already severely weakened by disease, suffered from shortages of food.

In 1648, the Iroquois launched a devastating attack that crushed the Huron Confederacy once and for all. Armed with guns they had acquired from the Dutch, large groups of Iroquois warriors began destroying entire Huron villages. Fleeing Hurons were given shelter in neighboring villages, but soon there was no place left to go. By the end of 1649, those who had not died from war, starvation, or disease were forced to leave Huronia and search for a new place to live. The Huron Confederacy was no more. ▲

*A Huron chief and his grandson, wearing ceremonial clothing, posed for this photograph in 1910.*

CHAPTER 6

# Wanderers

$A$fter the Huron Confederacy was defeated by the Iroquois, the members of the four tribes went their separate ways. Some decided to join Iroquois tribes. The Iroquois had lost a great many people to war and disease, and they welcomed their former enemies into their nation. About 1,000 Hurons settled among the Onondagas, one of the five Iroquois tribes. Others joined the Senecas, where they were reunited with relatives who had been captured. One Seneca village, Gandougarae, was composed entirely of former Hurons.

Most of the Hurons refused to join the Iroquois. Of these, one group traveled south to live with their trading partners, the Neutrals and the Petuns. Others fled to the island of Gahoendoe (now Christian Island) in Georgian Bay. Neither group was safe for long. This was just the first step in a long period of wandering.

The Hurons on Gahoendoe stayed only a year. There were not enough fields for them to plant crops, and they continued to be attacked by Iroquois warriors as they gathered berries and acorns. By winter they were starving.

Most of the Gahoendoe Hurons were Christians, and several Jesuit missionaries were traveling with them. These priests convinced the Hurons to go to Quebec. On June 10, 1650, a party of about 300 set out for Quebec. On the way they met a group of Hurons and French soldiers who were bringing food to Huronia. When the group was told that the Hurons had abandoned their homeland, they joined the Gahoendoe Hurons on their trip along the St. Lawrence River.

From 1650 to 1651, this group of Hurons, now about 400 strong, lived in Quebec with the support of the French. In 1651 they moved to the nearby island of Orleans, where more Hurons joined them. They survived by fishing and farming until 1656, when

*After the destruction of the Huron Confederacy in 1649, one group of Hurons fled to Gahoendoe Island in Georgian Bay. This group had to relocate many times before finally settling at Jeune Lorette in 1697.*

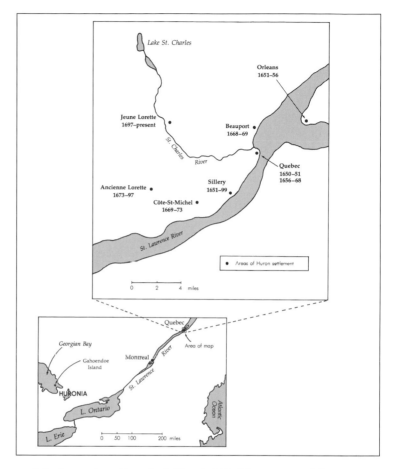

a Mohawk attack killed 70 Hurons. The survivors fled back to Quebec.

Knowing they could not survive many more such attacks, the remaining Hurons invited the Mohawks to *negotiate* a peace *treaty*. The Mohawks would end the fighting only if the Hurons moved to Mohawk villages to replace the people lost to war and disease. The Hurons felt that they had no alternative, so they agreed to join the Mohawks.

In the spring of 1657, a group of Mohawks and Onondagas arrived in Quebec to lead the Hurons south to Iroquois territory. Some of the Hurons joined the Onondagas, some joined the Mohawks, and some decided to remain in Quebec. After leaving Quebec, the Onondagas attacked the Hurons traveling with them, killing the men and taking the women captive. Those Hurons who had joined the Mohawks, however, were taken into Mohawk families and gradually adopted the ways of the Iroquois.

In 1667, the French made peace with the Iroquois. The Hurons who had remained in Quebec could finally leave the city without fear of attack. Numbering about 200, they moved first to Beauport, a town just north of Quebec. The following year they moved several miles south to a Jesuit *mission* in Côte-St-Michel. There they were joined by other Hurons, and by 1673 their population had reached 300. They then moved to a mission called Ancienne Lorette. Finally, in 1697, they found a permanent home near the mission of Jeune Lorette, eight miles north of Quebec.

The Hurons at Jeune Lorette tried to maintain their traditional lifestyle, but the area's sandy soil made farming difficult. The Hurons became even more dependent on trade with

*In 1701, the Hurons and other tribes in the area signed this peace treaty with the Iroquois. The chiefs signed the treaty by drawing the symbol of their clan; the signature of the Huron chief is in the bottom row at the left.*

the French, exchanging furs and lumber from the forest for food. Toward the end of the 18th century they found they could make more money by setting up workshops and selling moccasins, snowshoes, and canoes.

The British took control of New France in 1763 and renamed it Canada. In 1772, the British government gave the Hurons 1,352 acres of land known as Quarante Arpents, and in 1851 the Hurons were granted a 9,600-acre reserve called Cabane d'Automne. When the Hurons stopped using the land for hunting and fishing, they leased it to loggers. The Hurons sold the reserves in 1903 and 1904. The Indians gradually became more and more like their Canadian neighbors, living in single-family houses and speaking French.

The Hurons who had joined their trading partners the Petuns in 1649 underwent an even longer and more *arduous* journey. Less than a year after the Iroquois crushed the Huron Confederacy, they launched an equally fearsome attack on the Petuns. Together the remnants of the two groups began a series of difficult migrations.

They first moved to the island of Michilimackinac in what is now Michigan, where they settled near a group of friendly Ottawa Indians. They then moved west to

Huron Island (now called Rock Island) in Lake Michigan. By 1653, they moved farther west to avoid more Iroquois raids and settled along the Black River in Wisconsin. There they could farm, fish, and trap beavers. They quickly reestablished trade with the French, although this required an 800-mile trip to Quebec.

The Huron-Petuns soon made enemies in their new home. Their trappers sometimes hunted in the territory of the powerful Sioux tribe to the west. In order to avoid war with the Sioux, they moved again in 1661.

About 500 Huron-Petuns migrated north to Chequamegon, on the southern shore of Lake Superior, where they stayed for 10 years. When the French and their Indian allies made peace with the Iroquois, the Huron-Petuns decided to go back east to their former home near Michilimackinac. They stayed there until 1701, when they moved south to set up a village near the French trading post at Detroit. From there they made alliances with Indians to the south including the Lenape, Illinois, and Shawnee tribes.

According to Pierre de Charlevoix, a French explorer who visited Detroit in 1721, the Huron-Petuns were doing well in their new home. He wrote admiringly that "were it not for the Hurons the other Indians of [Detroit]

*The Huron-Petuns were driven from their land by Iroquois attacks in 1649. The path of their journey in search of a new homeland is charted here.*

NORTH DAKOTA

SOUTH DAKOTA

NEBRASKA

KANSAS

OKLAHOMA

TEXAS

MINNESOTA

IOWA

MISSOURI

ARKANSAS

MISSISSIPPI

WISCONSIN

ILLINOIS

INDIANA

MICHIGAN

OHIO

KENTUCKY

WEST VIRGINIA

VIRGINIA

PENNSYLVANIA

NEW YORK

CANADA

L. Superior

L. Huron

L. Michigan

L. Erie

L. Ontario

Chequamegon

Huron Island

Michilimackinac

HURONIA

Detroit

Upper Sandusky

Sandusky

1671

1650

1652

1658–65

1701–4

1843

1855–70

Black River

Mississippi

Missouri River

Neosho River

Arkansas River

Ohio River

River

Area of inset

Wyandot Reservation

Areas of Huron-Petun or Wyandot settlement

Modern state boundaries

Modern international boundaries

0  50  100    200  miles

KANSAS

MISSOURI

Quapaw

Peoria

Ottawa

Shawnee

Modoc

WYANDOT

Seneca

Neosho River

Spring River

must die of hunger. The Hurons . . . by means of their industry are in a condition not only to subsist without being beholden to anyone, but also to furnish a supply to their neighbors."

From 1754 to 1763, the Huron-Petuns fought alongside the French against the British in the French and Indian War. When the French lost, the British took control of the region. The Huron-Petuns became known by their English name, the Wyandots, a variation of their original name, Wendat. For a while Wyandot warriors continued to fight the British under the direction of the great Ottawa chief Pontiac. But with the French gone, the Wyandots soon began to trade with the British.

Because of this trade alliance, when the American Revolution broke out in 1776 the Wyandots fought with the British against the colonies. In 1782, an American force led by Colonel William Crawford captured and executed several Wyandot leaders. Before the troops departed, however, the Wyandots caught Colonel Crawford and burned him at the stake.

After the U.S. victory in 1783, American settlers began pouring into the Wyandots' land in what is now Ohio, and British settlers wanted their land in Canada. The Wyandots were forced to sign a number of treaties in which they gave up their territory in exchange for land elsewhere. With the Treaty of Detroit in 1790, the British promised the Wyandots money, a mission near Detroit, 23,630 acres of land north of Lake Erie, and 23,000 acres in Ontario near the present-day town of Anderdon. However, an 1800 treaty took back the mission land, and an 1836 treaty took back two-thirds of the land near Anderdon.

The Wyandots south of Lake Erie in what is now Sandusky, Ohio, banded with other tribes to fight the Americans. The British promised to support the Indians. In 1794, President George Washington sent soldiers to fight the Indians allied with the British. At the Battle of Fallen Timbers near present-day Toledo, Ohio, the English failed to join their Indian allies in the fighting, and U.S. troops crushed the Indians. The resulting Treaty of Greenville in 1795 *ceded* two-thirds of Indian hunting territory in Ohio to the United States. An 1805 treaty claimed one-third of the remaining land, and two years later the Indians had to give up most of the rest.

In 1830, the U.S. Congress passed the Indian Removal Act, which forced all eastern

Indians to move west to Indian Territory, in what is now Oklahoma, Kansas, and Nebraska. The Wyandots resisted moving west, but by 1843 they had been pressured to sell the last of their reservation land in Ohio, and all 700 agreed to move to Indian Territory. Not finding any land in Indian Territory they could survive on, they bought 25,260 acres in what is now Kansas from the Lenapes.

Even this land was not safe from the Americans, however. The Kansas-Nebraska Act opened new territory to American settlers, reducing Indian Territory to what is now Oklahoma. The Wyandots' land was now in Kansas Territory rather than Indian Territory. To encourage the Indians to give up their traditional ways and to live like American farmers, the U.S. government divided their land into small parcels called *allotments*, and each family was given a 40-acre tract.

About 200 Wyandots sold their allotments and moved to Indian Territory to avoid the rush of settlers. In 1858, they bought a 20,000-acre portion of the Senecas' reservation in northeastern Oklahoma. The U.S. Congress recognized this land as a Wyandot *reservation* in 1867, and the remaining Wyandots in Kansas were invited to sell their land and live on the reservation. There they could

*Philippe Gros-Louis, a resident of Wendake, makes snowshoes in a workshop on the reserve.*

give up the allotment system and resume their custom of sharing the land.

This situation did not last for long. In 1890, the Wyandots' reservation was taken away and each family received a tract of 160 acres. In 1907, the remains of Indian Territory officially became the state of Oklahoma. The Indians were encouraged to adopt American farming techniques, wear non-Indian clothing, and live in single-family houses.

Meanwhile, the Wyandots who had remained in Canada were also being forced to give up their old ways. In 1851, the reservation near Anderdon was divided up, and parcels were given to individual families. The Indian Act of 1876 had given the Indians the right to vote but taken away their reservation status. With no commonly held land, the Canadian Wyandot lost their sense of unity and adopted non-Indian customs.

The community that stayed at Jeune Lorette now lives on a reserve named Wendake, which means land of the Wendat. It maintains one of the highest standards of living of any Indian reserve in Canada. Wendake features many modern houses on attractive tree-lined streets. At the Huron Elementary School in Wendake, students are encouraged to study the Huron language.

In 1988, there were 959 Hurons living at Wendake, and 1,051 more lived outside the reserve. Wendake is governed by the elected Huron National Council. Many of the Hurons at Wendake still make their living selling handicrafts or making snowshoes and canoes; Wendake workshops produce 50,000 pairs of snowshoes and 3,000 canoes per year. Other Wendake Hurons own clothing or grocery stores or have jobs in Quebec, and some have become doctors, musicians, and artists.

Two people from Wendake have written books about Huron life. Marguerite Vincent's *La Nation Huronne* (The Huron Nation), published in 1984, tells the history of the Hurons. The book includes traditional songs and folktales and a dictionary of Huron words.

Max Gros-Louis's autobiography, *First Among the Hurons*, published in 1973, urges Hurons to demand justice for the theft of their land and other crimes committed against them by the Canadian government. Gros-Louis has been very active as a member of the Association of Indians of Quebec and as a founder of the National Indian Brotherhood of Canada, which supplies scholarships for Indian students and fights for Indian fishing rights and land claims. Gros-Louis served as chief councillor of the

Huron Nation from 1964 to 1984 and was elected again in 1987.

The 3,045 Wyandots in the United States do not live in one community, but instead are scattered across the country. The tribe does own a 188-acre tract near Wyandotte, Oklahoma, where 350 Wyandots live. Five hundred Wyandots live elsewhere in Oklahoma. The Wyandot Council meets at least once a month at the Wyandot Tribal Center in the town of Wyandotte. The council distributes money for education, home construction, and other needs.

The descendants of the Wendats have endured a long and tortuous struggle to survive in the more than 300 years since the fall of the powerful Huron Confederacy. Although the Wyandots in the United States and the Hurons in Canada have little contact with each other, both groups struggle to keep alive the remarkable culture they once shared.

Huron society succeeded in meeting not only the physical needs but the deepest spiritual longings of all its people. This legacy provides a humbling lesson for modern civilization, which for all of its wealth and technology cannot measure up to the Hurons' standards of sharing and generosity.

# GLOSSARY

| | |
|---|---|
| **allotment** | a small plot of land carved from a reservation and given to an individual family; also the policy of taking shared reservation land away from tribes and creating privately owned plots |
| **ambush** | to make a surprise attack from a place of hiding |
| **arduous** | extremely difficult and physically demanding |
| **blood feud** | lasting conflict between two groups resulting in a series of violent acts committed in revenge for previous attacks |
| **cannibalism** | eating human flesh, usually for ritual or religious purposes |
| **cede** | to surrender a piece of land to another group |
| **consensus** | the agreement of everyone in a group |
| **convert** | to give up one's religion and accept a different one, or to persuade someone else to do so |
| **domineering** | exercising power over another in a harsh or arrogant way |
| **influential** | able to sway the decisions of others; respected or admired |
| **Jesuit** | a member of a Catholic order started in 1523 by St. Ignatius of Loyola dedicated to missionary and educational work |
| **longhouse** | a building that houses several Huron families |
| **mission** | a settlement of people attempting to spread their religion in a foreign land |
| **missionary** | a person who travels to a foreign land to convert the native population to Christianity |
| **negotiate** | to discuss a problem or conflict and try to come to an agreement |
| **peninsula** | a piece of land that juts out from the coastline and is surrounded on three sides by water |
| **prosper** | to achieve success; to thrive and become wealthy |
| **reservation** | a piece of land defined by the federal government as the legal territory of an Indian tribe |
| **treaty** | an official agreement that settles a dispute between two or more groups |

# CHRONOLOGY

**c. 1000**    Ancestors of the Hurons begin planting corn and living in longhouses in present-day Ontario, Canada

**1534**    Jacques Cartier begins trading with Indians of New France

**1609**    Hurons have first contact with French when they are visited by Samuel de Champlain

**1610**    Iroquois begin trading with Dutch; rivalry with Hurons intensifies

**1635–40**    Half of Huron population dies in smallpox and measles epidemics

**1649**    Iroquois attacks destroy Huron Confederacy; some Hurons join Iroquois, some join Petuns, others eventually settle in Quebec

**1667**    French sign peace treaty with Iroquois; Hurons leave Quebec and begin series of migrations

**1697**    Hurons from Quebec settle at Jeune Lorette

**1701**    Huron-Petuns build villages near Detroit and Sandusky, Ohio

**1754–63**    Huron-Petuns and other local tribes join the French in the French and Indian War; Britain wins and New France becomes Canada; Huron-Petuns become known as Wyandots

**1776–83**    Wyandots fight alongside the British during the American Revolution

**1843**    Ohio Wyandots move to Indian Territory

**1876**    Canadian Wyandots are given allotments and made citizens; they gradually adopt non-Indian customs

**1890**    Wyandots' land in Indian Territory is divided into individually owned allotments

**1973**    Max Gros-Louis publishes *First Among the Hurons*, urging Hurons to demand justice for the theft of their land

**1984**    Marguerite Vincent's *La Nation Huronne* presents the history and legends of the Hurons

# INDEX

## ABOUT THE AUTHOR

MARTIN SCHWABACHER is the author of *Magic Johnson, Basketball Wizard* and *The Chumash Indians*, and he recently completed his first novel for young adults. He grew up in Minneapolis, Minnesota, and currently works as an editor and freelance writer in New York City.

## PICTURE CREDITS